PARENTING YOUR FIRST GRADER

A GUIDE TO MAKING THE MOST OF THE "LOOK AT ME!" PHASE

KRISTEN IVY AND REGGIE JOINER

PARENTING YOUR FIRST GRADER
A GUIDE TO MAKING THE MOST OF THE
"LOOK AT ME!" PHASE

Published by Orange, a division of The reThink Group, Inc.,
5870 Charlotte Lane, Suite 300,
Cumming, GA 30040 U.S.A.

©2017 Kristen Ivy and Reggie Joiner
Authors: Kristen Ivy and Reggie Joiner
Lead Editor: Karen Wilson
Editing Team: Melanie Williams, Hannah Crosby, Sherry Surratt

Art Direction: Ryan Boon and Hannah Crosby
Book Design: FiveStone and Sharon van Rossum

Printed in the United States of America
First Edition 2017
1 2 3 4 5 6 7 8 9 10

Special thanks to:

Jim Burns, Ph.D for guidance and consultation on having conversations about sexual integrity

Jon Acuff for guidance and consultation on having conversations about technological responsibility

Jean Sumner, MD for guidance and consultation on having conversations about healthy habits

Every educator, counselor, community leader, and researcher who invested in the Phase Project

TABLE OF CONTENTS

HOW TO USE THIS ~~BOOK~~ ~~JOURNAL~~ GUIDE

The guide you hold in your hand doesn't have very many words, but it does have a lot of ideas. Some of these ideas come from thousands of hours of research. Others come from parents, educators, and volunteers who spend every day with kids the same age as yours. This guide won't tell you everything about your kid, but it will tell you a few things about kids at this age.

The best way to use this guide is to take what these pages tell you about first graders and combine it with what you know is true about *your* first grader.

Let's sum it up:

THINGS ABOUT FIRST GRADERS +
THOUGHTS ABOUT *YOUR* FIRST GRADER =
YOUR GUIDE TO THE NEXT 52 WEEKS OF PARENTING

After each idea in this guide, there are pages with a few questions designed to prompt you to think about your kid, your family, and yourself as a parent. The only guarantee we give to parents who use this guide is this: You will mess up some things as a parent this year. Actually, that's a guarantee to every parent, regardless. But you, you picked up this book! You want to be a better parent. And that's what we hope this guide will do: help you parent your kid just a little better, simply because you paused to consider a few ideas that can help you make the most of this phase.

THE FIRST GRADE PHASE

In the world of education, we often group kindergartners, first graders, and second graders into a category called *early childhood*. Or, as I personally call them, the "fun" years. In this phase, there's very little drama or romantic distraction. Instead, it's the age where make-believe meets reality. Imagination pumps through the classroom so strongly you can almost feel it. And children discover they have the power to create a unique place in this world.

So, welcome to first grade! You're right in the heart of the sweetest years. Maybe that's why, as an elementary principal, I often find myself gravitating toward our first-grade hallway. There's just something special about this phase.
With one year of formal education behind them, most first graders begin to gain remarkable confidence, and enjoy exploring new and unfamiliar concepts.

First-grade classrooms also have the uncanny ability to celebrate growth. Sure, they're often graveyards for baby teeth and other things children must let go of to make room for growing up. But, there's also good reason to celebrate every time a child enthusiastically squeals, "I lost a tooth!" It's why we stop whatever we're doing, give them our full attention, and smile as we say: "My, my. You're growing up. Congratulations!" Even though we feel the bittersweet truth of it all.

Parents often ask how to support their children in first grade. The answer is simple: *Be with them.* Even though they might be starting to read, they still need you to read with them. Even though they like to be around friends, they still want to know you're right there *with* them. Even though they might be learning to do cartwheels, they do them much better when you're watching because you're *with* them. First graders are happiest when the adults they look up to are simply around—not just doing things for them, but doing things *with* them.

In truth, a parent's attention is the best thing for young children. This is especially true of first graders, who are learning how to see themselves by noticing the way *other people* see them.

Physiologically, a child's brain is actually wired for attention. Have you ever noticed your first grader repeating the same phrase over and over, or sometimes even acting out on purpose? Take comfort. Your kid is normal. They do these things because it feels better to receive negative attention than to be ignored. Your first grader craves your attention because it lets him know he matters.

So, what does this phase need most? *You.*

Life is moving fast. And, sometimes your time and attention may feel like the hardest thing to give. But, this is a phase that won't last forever. And, when you pay attention to the fun, unique individual your first grader is becoming, you'll discover the true joy of the first grade. And, when children know they're valued, it plants a seed of self-worth that will serve them well for years to come.

- SARAH ANN JENSEN
FOUNDER OF KIPP MEMPHIS PREPARATORY ELEMENTARY

"It's hard to connect with your child without first understanding where they are. As counselors and speakers at parenting events across the country, we spend a great deal of time teaching parents about development. To know *where* your child is—not just physically, but emotionally, socially, and spiritually, helps you to truly know and understand *who* your child is. And that understanding is the key to connecting. The Phase Guides give you the tools to do just that. Our wise friends Reggie and Kristen have put together an insightful, hopeful, practical, and literal year-by-year guide that will help you to understand and connect with your child at every age."

SISSY GOFF
M.ED., LPC-MHSP, DIRECTOR OF CHILD & ADOLESCENT COUNSELING AT DAYSTAR COUNSELING MINISTRIES IN NASHVILLE, TENNESSEE, SPEAKER AND AUTHOR OF ARE MY KIDS ON TRACK?

"These resources for parents are fantastically empowering, absolute in their simplicity, and completely doable in every way. The hard work that has gone into the Phase Project will echo through the next generation of children in powerful ways."

JENNIFER WALKER
RN BSN, AUTHOR AND FOUNDER OF MOMS ON CALL

"We all know where we want to end up in our parenting, but how to get there can seem like an unsolved mystery. Through the Phase Project series, Reggie Joiner and Kristen Ivy team up to help us out. The result is a resource that guides us through the different seasons of raising children, and provides a road map to parenting in such a way that we finish up with very few regrets."

SANDRA STANLEY
FOSTER CARE ADVOCATE, BLOGGER, WIFE TO ANDY STANLEY, MOTHER OF THREE

"Not only are the Phase Guides the most creative and well-thought-out guides to parenting I have ever encountered, these books are ESSENTIAL to my daily parenting. With a 13-year-old, 11-year-old, and 9-year-old at home, I am swimming in their wake of daily drama and delicacy. These books are a reminder to enjoy every second. Because it's just a phase."

CARLOS WHITTAKER
AUTHOR, SPEAKER, FATHER OF THREE

"As the founder of Minnie's Food Pantry, I see thousands of people each month with children who will benefit from the advice, guidance, and nuggets of information on how to celebrate and understand the phases of their child's life. Too often we feel like we're losing our mind when sweet little Johnny starts to change his behavior into a person we do not know. I can't wait to start implementing the principles of these books with my clients to remind them . . . it's just a phase."

CHERYL JACKSON
FOUNDER OF MINNIE'S FOOD PANTRY, AWARD-WINNING PHILANTHROPIST, AND GRANDMOTHER

"I began exploring this resource with my counselor hat on, thinking how valuable this will be for the many parents I spend time with in my office. I ended up taking my counselor hat off and putting on my parent hat. Then I kept thinking about friends who are teachers, coaches, youth pastors, and children's ministers, who would want this in their hands. What a valuable resource the Orange team has given us to better understand and care for the kids and adolescents we love. I look forward to sharing it broadly."

DAVID THOMAS
LMSW, DIRECTOR OF FAMILY COUNSELING, DAYSTAR COUNSELING MINISTRIES, SPEAKER AND AUTHOR OF ARE MY KIDS ON TRACK? AND WILD THINGS: THE ART OF NURTURING BOYS

"I have always wished someone would hand me a manual for parenting. Well, the Phase Guides are more than what I wished for. They guide, inspire, and challenge me as a parent—while giving me incredible insight into my children at each age and phase. Our family will be using these every year!"

COURTNEY DEFEO
AUTHOR OF IN THIS HOUSE, WE WILL GIGGLE, MOTHER OF TWO

"As I speak to high school students and their parents, I always wonder to myself: What would it have been like if they had better seen what was coming next? What if they had a guide that would tell them what to expect and how to be ready? What if they could anticipate what is predictable about the high school years before they actually hit? These Phase Guides give a parent that kind of preparation so they can have a plan when they need it most."

JOSH SHIPP
AUTHOR, TEEN EXPERT, AND YOUTH SPEAKER

"The Phase Guides are incredibly creative, well researched, and filled with inspirational actions for everyday life. Each age-specific guide is catalytic for equipping parents to lead and love their kids as they grow up. I'm blown away and deeply encouraged by the content and by its creators. I highly recommend Phase resources for all parents, teachers, and influencers of children. This is the stuff that challenges us and changes our world. Get them. Read them. And use them!"

DANIELLE STRICKLAND
OFFICER WITH THE SALVATION ARMY, AUTHOR, SPEAKER, MOTHER OF TWO

"It's true that parenting is one of life's greatest joys but it is not without its challenges. If we're honest, parenting can sometimes feel like trying to choreograph a dance to an ever-changing beat. It can be clumsy and riddled with well-meaning missteps. If parenting is a dance, this Parenting Guide is a skilled instructor refining your technique and helping you move gracefully to a steady beat. For those of us who love to plan ahead, this guide will help you anticipate what's to come so you can be poised and ready to embrace the moments you want to enjoy."

TINA NAIDOO
MSSW, LCSW EXECUTIVE DIRECTOR, THE POTTER'S HOUSE OF DALLAS, INC.

52

WEEKS

—

TO PARENT YOUR

FIRST GRADER

WHEN YOU SEE
HOW MUCH

Time

YOU HAVE LEFT

—

YOU TEND TO DO

More

WITH THE TIME
YOU HAVE NOW.

THERE ARE APPROXIMATELY

936 WEEKS

FROM THE TIME A BABY IS BORN UNTIL THEY GROW UP AND MOVE TO WHATEVER IS NEXT.

It may seem hard to believe, but on the day your child starts first grade, you only have 624 weeks remaining. And while things like cell phone contracts and learners permits still seem far away, you're starting to realize your kid is growing up faster than you ever dreamed.

That's why every week counts. Of course, each week might not feel significant. There may be weeks this year when all you feel like you accomplished was getting them fed, bathed, and to bed on time (most nights). That's okay.

Take a deep breath.
You don't have to get everything done this week.

But what happens in your child's life week after week, year after year, adds up over time. So, it might be a good idea to put a number to your weeks.

MEASURE IT OUT.

Write down the number of weeks that have already passed since your child was born. Then write down the number of weeks you have left before they graduate high school.

HINT: If you want a little help counting it out, you can download the free Parent Cue app on all mobile platforms.

_____

_____

_____

CREATE A VISUAL COUNTDOWN.

Find a jar and fill it with one marble for each week you have remaining with your child. Then make a habit of removing one marble every week as a reminder to make the most your time. Where can you place your visual countdown so you will see it frequently?

_____

_____

_____

_____

_____

Which day of the week is best for you to remove a marble?

_____

_____

_____

Is there anything you want to do each week as you remove a marble? *(Examples: say a prayer, play a game, retell one favorite memory from this past week)*

_____

_____

_____

_____

_____

_____

_____

_____

_____

_____

_____

_____

_____

EVERY PHASE IS A

TIMEFRAME

IN A KID'S LIFE

WHEN YOU CAN

LEVERAGE

DISTINCTIVE

OPPORTUNITIES

TO INFLUENCE

THEIR

future.

YOU ONLY HAVE
52 WEEKS
WITH YOUR FIRST GRADER

while they are still in first grade.
Then they will be in second grade,
and you will never know them as a first grader again.

Or, to say it another way:
Before you know it, your kid will grow up a little more and . . .
say a word you didn't know they knew.
introduce you to a friend you didn't know they had.
ask a homework question you can't answer from memory.

The point is this: The phase you are in now has remarkable potential. And before the end of first grade, there are some distinctive opportunities you don't want to miss. So, as you count down the next 52 weeks, pay attention to what makes these weeks uniquely different from the time you've already spent together and the weeks you will have when they move on to the next phase.

What are some things you have noticed about your first grader in this phase that you really enjoy?

_____

_____

_____

_____

_____

_____

_____

_____

_____

_____

_____

_____

_____

_____

_____

_____

_____

What is something new you are learning as a parent during this phase?

_____

_____

_____

_____

_____

_____

_____

_____

_____

_____

_____

_____

_____

_____

_____

_____

_____

_____

_____

_____

_____

FIRST GRADE

—

THE PHASE WHEN
UNFILTERED WORDS
MAKE YOU LAUGH,
SCHOOL DROP-OFF
MAKES YOU CRY, AND
LIFE BECOMES A STAGE
WHERE YOUR KID SHOUTS,

"Look at me!"

GET READY FOR MEMORABLE STATEMENTS.

Your child is now a sophisticated conversationalist—at least in their mind. With one year of school under their belt, they are quickly becoming more confident in their opinions and observations. You may be amazed and entertained by all the profound and uncensored things they say, like, "I stink on the stairs when I eat brown beans."

ADJUST FOR A CULTURAL SHIFT—SCHOOL.

It's only the second year, and your kid is still adjusting to less playtime, more early-morning alarm clocks, and an even higher demand for focused attention. It's still important to give after-school opportunities for a little unstructured play, a chance to skip and run, to throw and catch, and to use their imagination.

GIVE SOME UNDIVIDED ATTENTION.

The average first grade class has twenty kids—some even as cute and smart as your own. But first graders are hungry for individualized adult attention and approval. So when it's the end of the day and your first grader keeps asking, "Look at me," give them your attention as freely and as often as possible.

THIS

YEAR

YOUR

FIRST

GRADER

IS

changing.

PHYSICALLY

- Loses incisor teeth (6-8 years)
- Grows two to three inches and gains an average of five pounds
- Able to swim, skip, gallop, and move to the beat of music
- Draws with considerable detail
- Needs 10-12 hours of sleep each night

SOCIALLY

- Wants to finish first (may be highly competitive)
- Can be bossy or critical of others
- Needs guidance taking turns and losing well
- May have a best friend (or may not)

MENTALLY

- Can focus on one activity for 5–15 minutes
- Beginning to understand ironic humor and tell simple jokes
- Often very ambitious and motivated to learn
- Beginning to logically interpret cause and effect

EMOTIONALLY

- Tends to be enthusiastic
- Benefits from relaxation techniques (take a deep breath)
- Expresses feelings better through play and art (rather than in words)
- Deals with fear and anxiety by distracting themselves
- Highly sensitive to harsh criticism, tone, and body language

What are some changes you are noticing in your first grader?

_____

_____

_____

_____

_____

_____

_____

You may disagree with some of the characteristics we've shared about first graders. That's because every first grader is unique. What makes your first grader different from first graders in general?

_____

_____

_____

_____

_____

_____

_____

_____

What do you want to remember about this year with your first grader?

Mark this page. Throughout the year, write down a few simple things you don't want to forget. If you want to be really thorough, there just happens to be about 52 blank lines. Some weeks you may spend so much time trying to get them to pick up their things that you forget to write down a memory. And that's okay.

SIX
THINGS

EVERY KID
NEEDS

YOUR KID
NEEDS **6** THINGS
OVER TIME

LOVE
STORIES
WORK
WORDS
PEOPLE
FUN

OVER THE NEXT 624 WEEKS YOUR CHILD WILL NEED MANY THINGS.

Some of the things your kid needs will change from phase to phase, but there are six things every kid needs at every phase. In fact, these things may be the most important things you give your kid.

EVERY KID, AT EVERY PHASE, NEEDS . . .

♡ LOVE
to give them a
sense of WORTH.

📖 STORIES
to give them a bigger
PERSPECTIVE.

🏋 WORK
to give them
PURPOSE.

♟ FUN
to give them
CONNECTION.

👥 PEOPLE
to give them
BELONGING.

💬 WORDS
to give them
DIRECTION.

The next few pages are designed to help you think about how you will give your child these six things, right now—while they are in first grade.

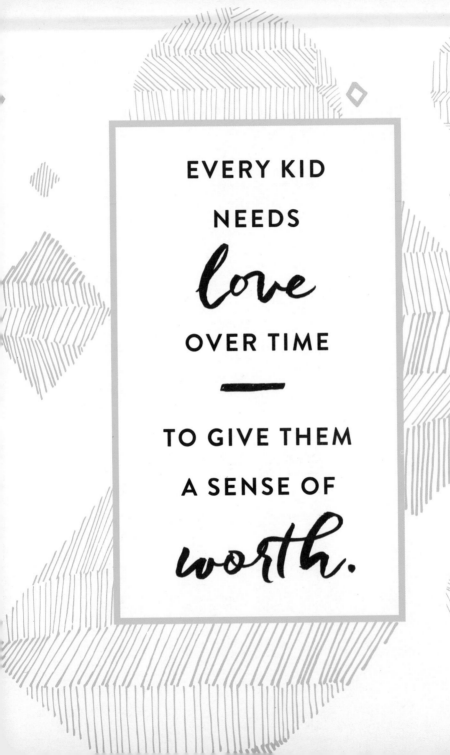

EVERY KID

NEEDS

love

OVER TIME

—

TO GIVE THEM

A SENSE OF

worth.

♡ ONE QUESTION YOUR FIRST GRADER IS ASKING

Your first grader's schedule may be picking up pace—from bus rides to recreational sports to after-school programs. But with all the increasing opportunities to try new things, don't miss what your first grader needs most.

Your first grader is asking one major question:

"DO I HAVE YOUR ATTENTION?"

Your first grader needs to know you see their efforts, their ideas, their accomplishments, and their failures. Being your first grader's parent probably isn't the only thing you have going on. So remember this—in order to give your first grader the love and attention they need, you need to do one thing:

ENGAGE their interests.

When you engage your first grader's interests, you . . .
communicate that their ideas have value,
establish that their efforts are significant,
and demonstrate that they are worth loving.

You are probably doing more than you realize to show your first grader just how much you love them. Make a list of the ways you already show up to consistently engage your child's interests.

🏆 You may need to look at this list on a bad day to remember what a great parent you are.

_____

_____

_____

_____

_____

_____

_____

_____

_____

_____

_____

_____

_____

Engaging your child's interests requires paying attention to what they like. What does your first grader seem to enjoy the most right now?

_____

_____

_____

_____

_____

_____

_____

_____

_____

_____

_____

_____

_____

_____

_____

_____

_____

_____

_____

_____

It's impossible to love anyone with the attention a first grader requires unless you have a little time for yourself. What can you do to refuel each week so you are able to give your first grader the love they need?

_____

_____

_____

_____

_____

_____

_____

_____

_____

_____

_____

_____

_____

_____

_____

_____

_____

Who do you have around you supporting you this year?

_____

_____

_____

_____

_____

_____

_____

_____

_____

_____

_____

_____

_____

_____

_____

_____

_____

_____

_____

_____

EVERY KID

NEEDS

stories

OVER TIME

—

TO GIVE THEM

A BIGGER

perspective.

BOOKS TO READ
WITH YOUR FIRST GRADER

MRS. NELSON IS BACK
by Harry G. Allard Jr. and
James Marshall

FLAT STANLEY (SERIES)
by Jeff Brown

**NANA UPSTAIRS AND
NANA DOWNSTAIRS**
by Tomie dePaola

WAITING
by Kevin Henkes

**THE FANTASTIC FLYING BOOKS
OF MR. MORRIS LESSMORE**
by William Joyce

**THE LION, THE WITCH, AND
THE WARDROBE**
by C.S. Lewis

MRS. PIGGLE-WIGGLE (SERIES)
by Betty MacDonald

ENEMY PIE
by Derek Munson

THE BOOK WITH NO PICTURES
by B.J. Novak

MAGIC TREE HOUSE (SERIES)
by Mary Pope Osborne

THE DOT
by Peter H. Reynolds

UNIQUE MONIQUE
by Maria Rousaki

POEM COLLECTIONS
by Shel Silverstein

A BAD CASE OF STRIPES
by David Shannon

JUMANJI
by Chris Van Allsburg

IRA SLEEPS OVER
by Bernard Waber

NATE THE GREAT (SERIES)
by Marjorie Weinman Sharmat

CHARLOTTE'S WEB
by E.B. White

ELEPHANT AND PIGGIE (SERIES)
by Mo Willems

THE VELVETEEN RABBIT
by Margery Williams

Tell your first grader's story. Do you have a photo album, a website, or a baby book? What are some ways you can preserve and retell the story of your kid's first years?

_____

_____

_____

_____

_____

_____

_____

_____

_____

_____

_____

_____

_____

_____

_____

_____

_____

_____

Tell your story. *(Okay, maybe not all of it right now.)* What are some life stories that you can share with your first grader?

_____

_____

_____

_____

_____

_____

_____

_____

_____

_____

_____

_____

_____

_____

_____

_____

_____

_____

Tell your family story. What do you want to record now so you can share it with your first grader later? Consider starting a family journal, a video archive, a travel scrapbook, or a drawer of things connected to special memories. Write down some ideas below that might fit your family's values and style.

_____

_____

_____

_____

_____

_____

_____

_____

_____

_____

_____

_____

_____

_____

_____

EVERY KID

NEEDS

work

OVER TIME

—

TO GIVE

THEM

purpose.

WORK YOUR
FIRST GRADER CAN DO

TIE SHOES
(pretty well)

**BRUSH TEETH
INDEPENDENTLY**

BATHE
(may still need help rinsing
their hair)

DO HOMEWORK
(with assistance)

**WRITE CARDS AND
THANK YOU NOTES**

**SORT TOYS AND PUT
THEM AWAY**

MAKE A PB&J SANDWICH

**FOLD AND PUT
AWAY TOWELS**
(if "away" is somewhere 2 feet
off the ground)

**PUT CLOTHES
ON HANGERS**

TAKE CARE OF PETS

BRING IN THE MAIL

REFILL THE TOILET PAPER

What are some jobs you can give to your first grader?

_____

_____

_____

_____

_____

_____

_____

_____

_____

_____

_____

_____

_____

_____

_____

_____

_____

_____

Some days it's easier than others to motivate your first grader to do their work. What are some strategies that tend to keep your first grader motivated?

HINT: Maybe try a few things like, "You can pick the book we read / movie we watch next."

_____

_____

_____

_____

_____

_____

_____

_____

_____

_____

_____

_____

_____

_____

_____

_____

_____

_____

What are things you hope your first grader will be able to do independently in the next phase?

_____

_____

_____

_____

_____

_____

_____

_____

_____

_____

_____

_____

_____

_____

_____

_____

_____

_____

_____

How are you helping them develop those skills now?

_____

_____

_____

_____

_____

_____

_____

_____

_____

_____

_____

_____

_____

_____

_____

_____

_____

_____

_____

_____

_____

_____

EVERY KID

NEEDS

fun

OVER TIME

—

TO GIVE

THEM

connection.

WAYS TO HAVE FUN WITH YOUR FIRST GRADER

GAMES:

HI HO! CHERRY-O®

TROUBLE®

SORRY®

CHECKERS

CHESS

CHINESE CHECKERS

UNO®, WAR, OLD MAID (CARD GAMES)

OPERATION®

MOUSETRAP®

TIC-TAC-TOE

DOMINOS

BINGO

CONNECT 4®

SPOT IT! ®

ACTIVITIES:

ART WITH MARKERS OR TEMPURA PAINT

SWING, CLIMB, AND SLIDE

SWIM AND PLAY IN THE WATER

RED LIGHT, GREEN LIGHT

WATER BALLOONS

CHINESE JUMP ROPE

CATCH FIREFLIES

LEAPFROG

BALLOON STOMPS

RELAY RACES

HUMAN KNOTS

LEGOS®

BEANBAG TOSS

MARBLE RUNS

PIÑATA WITH CANDY

50-PIECE JIGSAW PUZZLES

SIMON SAYS

NATURE WALKS

What are some games and activities you and your first grader enjoy?

When are the best times of the day, or week, for you to set aside to just have fun with your first grader?

_____

_____

_____

_____

_____

_____

_____

_____

_____

_____

_____

_____

_____

_____

_____

_____

_____

_____

_____

Some days are *extra* fun days. What are some ways you want to celebrate the special days coming up this year?

CHILD'S BIRTHDAY

_____

_____

_____

_____

_____

_____

_____

_____

_____

_____

_____

_____

_____

_____

_____

_____

_____

HOLIDAYS

EVERY KID

NEEDS

people

OVER TIME

—

TO GIVE

THEM

belonging.

ADULTS WHO MIGHT INFLUENCE YOUR FIRST GRADER

PARENTS

NEIGHBORS

CHURCH LEADERS

GRANDPARENTS

PARENT'S FRIENDS

COACHES

AUNTS & UNCLES

FIRST GRADE TEACHER

BABYSITTERS

List at least five adults who have influence in your first grader's life right now.

🔑 HINT: They're probably the adults your first grader talks about most.

_____

_____

_____

_____

_____

_____

_____

_____

_____

_____

_____

_____

_____

_____

_____

_____

_____

What is one way these adults can help you and your first grader this year?

_____

_____

_____

_____

_____

_____

_____

_____

_____

_____

_____

_____

_____

_____

_____

_____

_____

_____

_____

What are a few ways you could show these adults appreciation for the significant role they play in your child's life?

_____

_____

_____

_____

_____

_____

_____

_____

_____

_____

_____

_____

_____

_____

_____

_____

_____

_____

EVERY KID

NEEDS

words

OVER TIME

—

TO GIVE

THEM

direction.

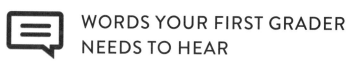

WORDS YOUR FIRST GRADER NEEDS TO HEAR

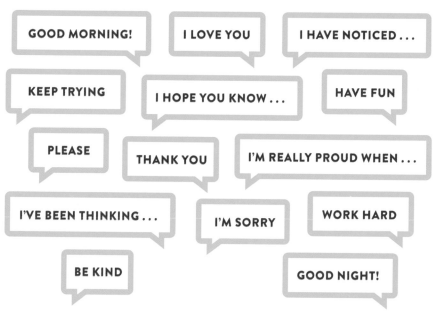

GOOD MORNING!

I LOVE YOU

I HAVE NOTICED . . .

KEEP TRYING

I HOPE YOU KNOW . . .

HAVE FUN

PLEASE

THANK YOU

I'M REALLY PROUD WHEN . . .

I'VE BEEN THINKING . . .

I'M SORRY

WORK HARD

BE KIND

GOOD NIGHT!

Don't forget: your first grader is still learning vocabulary. Here are a few ways you can help:

1.

Talk to your first grader— the more, the better.

2.

When they talk, make eye contact.

3.

Use school vocabulary words in everyday contexts.

4.

Read, sing, or make up rhymes.

5.

Talk about new words when they see or hear them.

If words over time give a kid direction, what word (or words) describes your hopes for your first grader in this phase?

DETERMINED	MOTIVATED	GENTLE
ENCOURAGING	INTROSPECTIVE	PASSIONATE
SELF-ASSURED	ENTHUSIASTIC	PATIENT
ASSERTIVE	JOYFUL	FORGIVING
DARING	ENTERTAINING	CREATIVE
INSIGHTFUL	INDEPENDENT	WITTY
COMPASSIONATE	OBSERVANT	AMBITIOUS
AMIABLE	SENSITIVE	HELPFUL
EASY-GOING	ENDEARING	AUTHENTIC
DILIGENT	ADVENTUROUS	INVENTIVE
PROACTIVE	HONEST	DEVOTED
OPTIMISTIC	CURIOUS	GENUINE
FEARLESS	DEPENDABLE	ATTENTIVE
AFFECTIONATE	GENEROUS	HARMONIOUS
COURAGEOUS	COMMITTED	EMPATHETIC
CAUTIOUS	RESPONSIBLE	COURAGEOUS
DEVOTED	TRUSTWORTHY	FLEXIBLE
INQUISITIVE	THOUGHTFUL	CAREFUL
PATIENT	LOYAL	NURTURING
OPEN-MINDED	KIND	RELIABLE

Where can you place those words in your home so they will remind you what you want for your child this year?

_____

_____

_____

_____

_____

_____

_____

_____

_____

_____

_____

_____

_____

_____

_____

_____

_____

_____

_____

_____

_____

The words we use determine the way we think. Are there words you have chosen not to say *(or not to say often)*? What do you want for your kid to know about these words, and how do you want them to respond if they hear them?

FOUR CONVERSATIONS

TO HAVE IN THIS PHASE

WHEN YOU KNOW
WHERE YOU WANT
TO GO,

AND YOU KNOW
WHERE YOU ARE
NOW,

YOU CAN ALWAYS
DO SOMETHING

TO MOVE IN A
BETTER DIRECTION.

OVER THE NEXT 624 WEEKS OF YOUR CHILD'S LIFE, SOME CONVERSATIONS MAY MATTER MORE THAN OTHERS.

**WHAT YOU SAY,
FOR EXAMPLE,
REGARDING . . .**
Star Wars

Shark Attacks

and Justin Timberlake

**MIGHT HAVE LESS
IMPACT ON THEIR
FUTURE THAN WHAT
YOU SAY REGARDING . . .**
Health

Sex

Technology

or Faith.

The next pages are about the conversations that matter most. On the left page is a destination—what you might want to be true in your kid's life 624 weeks from now. On the right page is a goal for conversations with your first grader and a few suggestions about what you might want to say.

Healthy habits

—

LEARNING TO STRENGTHEN MY BODY THROUGH EXERCISE, NUTRITION, AND SELF-ADVOCACY

THIS YEAR YOU WILL

DEVELOP POSITIVE ROUTINES

SO YOUR CHILD WILL ENJOY EATING WELL AND EXERCISING OFTEN.

Maintain a good relationship with your pediatrician, and schedule a well visit at least once per year. You can also begin to develop healthy habits for your first grader with a few simple words.

SAY THINGS LIKE . . .

LET'S GO ON A HIKE.

I LOVE TO WATCH YOU RUN / SWIM / RIDE YOUR BIKE!

WHAT WOULD YOU LIKE FOR DINNER THIS WEEK?
(Plan meals ahead of time and encourage a healthy variety.)

LET'S DRINK SOME MORE WATER.
(Kids need five 8oz cups of water per day.)

CAN YOU CUT OUT THE BISCUITS?
(Teach cooking basics.)

BREAKFAST IS THE MOST IMPORTANT MEAL OF THE DAY.

What are some activities you can do with your first grader that require a little bit of exercise? *(They may not call it exercise, but if you get a little winded that counts.)*

_____

_____

_____

_____

_____

_____

_____

_____

_____

_____

_____

_____

_____

_____

_____

_____

_____

_____

Kids who cook learn about what ingredients are in the things they eat. What are some simple ways your first grader can help you in the kitchen?

_____

_____

_____

_____

_____

_____

_____

_____

_____

_____

_____

_____

_____

_____

_____

_____

_____

_____

_____

Who will help you monitor and improve your first grader's health?

_____

_____

_____

_____

_____

_____

_____

_____

_____

_____

_____

_____

_____

_____

_____

_____

_____

_____

What are your own health goals for this year? How can you improve the habits in your own life—*you know, even though some days the most exercise you get is running to the bus stop when you're late?*

_____

_____

_____

_____

_____

_____

_____

_____

_____

_____

_____

_____

_____

_____

_____

_____

_____

_____

Sexual integrity

—

GUARDING MY
POTENTIAL FOR
INTIMACY THROUGH
APPROPRIATE
BOUNDARIES
AND MUTUAL
RESPECT

THIS YEAR YOU WILL

INFORM THEM ABOUT HOW THINGS WORK (KIND OF)

SO YOUR CHILD WILL UNDERSTAND BIOLOGY AND BUILD SOCIAL SKILLS.

Your first grader may be asking some questions—or they may not. It's up to you to determine just how much they are ready to hear when it comes to details about sex. In this phase, the most important thing is to give simple answers, continue coaching personal boundaries, and keep the conversations casual.

SAY THINGS LIKE . . .

GOD MADE YOUR BODY, AND WE WANT TO TAKE GOOD CARE OF IT.

"CAN WE TALK MORE ABOUT THIS ANOTHER TIME?"
(Always finish the conversation with room to pick it back up again later.)

I'M SO GLAD YOU ASKED ME.

"CAN YOU GIVE YOUR FRIEND SOME SPACE?"

"IT'S ALWAYS OKAY TO TELL SOMEONE 'NO' IF YOU DON'T WANT THEM TO TOUCH YOU."

"TOUCHING IS NEVER SECRET."

"IF SOMEONE TOUCHES YOU AND YOU DON'T LIKE IT, COME AND TELL ME RIGHT AWAY."

When it comes to your child's sexuality, what do you hope is true for them 624 weeks from now?

_____

_____

_____

_____

_____

_____

_____

_____

_____

_____

_____

_____

_____

_____

_____

_____

_____

_____

_____

Write down a few things you want to communicate to your first grader about their body in this phase. *(They won't remember it all after one talk. It will take many talks—over time—to communicate what you want them to know.)*

What do you want to communicate to your first grader about sex when the time comes to talk about it in more detail? *(You may choose the time and place of the conversation, or they may ask you before you planned—so you might as well give it a little thought ahead of time.)*

_____

_____

_____

_____

_____

_____

_____

_____

_____

_____

_____

_____

_____

_____

_____

_____

_____

_____

_____

_____

_____

_____

_____

_____

_____

_____

_____

_____

_____

_____

_____

_____

_____

_____

_____

For a little help imagining what to say, check out resources like *How God Makes Babies* by Dr. Jim Burns, *Simple Truths* by Mary Flo Ridley, or *Before I Was Born* by Stan and Brenna Jones.

Technological responsibility

—

LEVERAGING THE POTENTIAL OF ONLINE EXPERIENCES TO ENHANCE MY OFFLINE COMMUNITY AND SUCCESS

THIS YEAR YOU WILL

EXPLORE THE POSSIBILITIES

SO YOUR CHILD WILL UNDERSTAND CORE VALUES AND BUILD ONLINE SKILLS.

Your first grader is gaining digital proficiency every day—most schools schedule some engagement with technology. But, even though your kid is a digital native, they still need an adult guide as they continue to explore all the great things they can do with technology.

SAY THINGS LIKE . . .

"NEVER USE GOOGLE (OR ANY SEARCH ENGINE) ALONE."
(Know when they are on a device and what they are using it to do.)

"LET ME SEE WHAT YOU DID."
(Show interest in what they do with technology.)

"YOU HAVE TEN MORE MINUTES AND THEN IT'S TIME TO PUT THE IPAD AWAY."
(Set limits for screen time.)

I DON'T KNOW, BUT WE CAN LOOK THAT UP TOGETHER.
(use technology to enhance your conversations.)

YOU NEED TO ASK BEFORE YOU USE THE COMPUTER.

"I'M TEXTING GRANDMA TO ASK A QUESTION."
(Talk openly about technology as you use it.)

"SIRI DOESN'T ALWAYS KNOW WHAT WE ARE ASKING."
(Turn on safe search, and don't let Siri answer your first grader's questions.)

When it comes to your child's engagement with technology, what do you hope is true for them 624 weeks from now?

_____

_____

_____

_____

_____

_____

_____

_____

_____

_____

_____

_____

_____

_____

_____

_____

_____

_____

_____

_____

What rules do you have for digital devices in your family? If you don't have any, what are two or three you might want to set for your first grader?

_____

_____

_____

_____

_____

_____

_____

_____

_____

_____

_____

_____

_____

_____

_____

_____

_____

_____

_____

What are your own personal values and disciplines when it comes to leveraging technology? Are there ways you want to improve your own savvy, skill, or responsibility in this area?

_____

_____

_____

_____

_____

_____

_____

_____

_____

_____

_____

_____

_____

_____

_____

_____

_____

_____

Authentic faith

—

**TRUSTING JESUS
IN A WAY THAT
TRANSFORMS HOW
I LOVE GOD,
MYSELF,
AND THE REST
OF THE WORLD**

THIS YEAR YOU WILL

PROVOKE DISCOVERY

SO YOUR CHILD WILL TRUST GOD'S CHARACTER AND EXPERIENCE GOD'S FAMILY.

Your first grader may be starting to read and enjoy books. So, this is a great year to purchase a kid's Bible. Look for one that is the full text, in an easy-to-read translation like the NIrV. You will need to read it to them for now. Continue having other faith conversations as you go about your days together.

SAY THINGS LIKE . . .

"ARE YOU SCARED? LET'S TALK TO GOD ABOUT IT."

"ISN'T THAT WONDERFUL? LET'S THANK GOD FOR IT."

"YOU CAN TRUST GOD NO MATTER WHAT."

"YOU NEED TO MAKE THE WISE CHOICE."

"YOU SHOULD TREAT OTHERS THE WAY YOU WANT TO BE TREATED."

"A FRIEND LOVES AT ALL TIMES. HE IS THERE TO HELP WHEN TROUBLE COMES." Proverbs 17:17
(Repeat simple Bible verses.)

"THE BIBLE HAS TWO PARTS, THE OLD TESTAMENT AND THE NEW TESTAMENT."
(Talk about the Bible.)

"LET'S TAKE A NEW BOOK TO YOUR FRIEND WHO STAYED HOME SICK TODAY."
(Involve them in serving friends and neighbors.)

When it comes to your child's faith, what do you hope is true for them 624 weeks from now?

_____

_____

_____

_____

_____

_____

_____

_____

_____

_____

_____

_____

_____

_____

_____

_____

_____

_____

What adults are helping influence and develop your first grader's faith?

_____

_____

_____

_____

_____

_____

_____

_____

_____

_____

_____

_____

_____

_____

_____

_____

_____

_____

_____

What routines or habits do you have in your own life that are stretching your faith?

_____

_____

_____

_____

_____

_____

_____

_____

_____

_____

_____

_____

_____

_____

_____

_____

_____

_____

THE

rhythm

OF YOUR

WEEK

—

WILL SHAPE

THE VALUES

IN YOUR

home.

NOW THAT YOU HAVE FILLED THIS BOOK WITH IDEAS AND GOALS, IT MAY SEEM AS IF YOU WILL NEVER HAVE TIME TO GET IT ALL DONE.

Actually, you have *624 weeks*.

And every week has potential.

The secret to making the most of this phase with your first grader is to take advantage of the time you already have. Create a rhythm to your weeks by leveraging these four times together.

Be a coach.
Instill purpose by starting the day with encouraging words.

Be a friend.
Interpret life during informal conversations as you travel.

Be a teacher.
Establish values with intentional conversations while you eat together.

Be a counselor.
Strengthen your relationship through heart conversations at the end of the day.

What are some of your favorite routines with your first grader?

_____

_____

_____

_____

_____

_____

_____

_____

_____

_____

_____

_____

_____

_____

_____

_____

_____

_____

Write down any other thoughts or questions about parenting your first grader.

YOU HAVE

APPROXIMATELY

624 WEEKS.

IT'S JUST
A PHASE
SO DON'T
MISS IT.

ABOUT THE AUTHORS

KRISTEN IVY @kristen_ivy

Kristen Ivy is executive director of the Phase Project. She and her husband, Matt, are in the preschool and elementary phases with three kids: Sawyer, Hensley, and Raleigh.

Kristen earned her Bachelors of Education from Baylor University in 2004 and received a Master of Divinity from Mercer University in 2009. She worked in the public school system as a high school biology and English teacher, where she learned firsthand the importance of influencing the next generation.

Kristen is also the President at Orange and has played an integral role in the development of the elementary, middle school, and high school curriculum and has shared her experiences at speaking events across the country. She is the co-author of *Playing for Keeps*, *Creating a Lead Small Culture*, *It's Just a Phase*, and *Don't Miss It*.

REGGIE JOINER @reggiejoiner

Reggie Joiner is founder and CEO of the reThink Group and co-founder of the Phase Project. He and his wife, Debbie, have reared four kids into adulthood. They now also have two grandchildren.

The reThink Group (also known as Orange) is a non-profit organization whose purpose is to influence those who influence the next generation. Orange provides resources and training for churches and organizations that create environments for parents, kids, and teenagers.

Before starting the reThink Group in 2006, Reggie was one of the founders of North Point Community Church. During his 11 years with Andy Stanley, Reggie was the executive director of family ministry, where he developed a new concept for relevant ministry to children, teenagers, and married adults. Reggie has authored and co-authored more than 10 books including: *Think Orange, Seven Practices of Effective Ministry, Parenting Beyond Your Capacity, Playing for Keeps, Lead Small, Creating a Lead Small Culture*, and his latest, *A New Kind of Leader* and *Don't Miss It*.

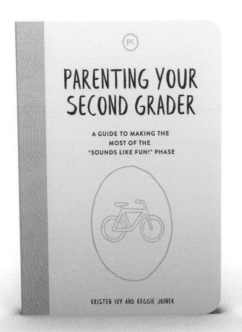

PARENTING YOUR SECOND GRADER

A GUIDE TO MAKING THE MOST OF THE "SOUNDS LIKE FUN!" PHASE

KRISTEN IVY AND REGGIE JOINER

MAKE THE MOST OF EVERY PHASE IN YOUR CHILD'S LIFE

The guide in your hand is one of an eighteen-part series.

So, unless you've figured out a way to freeze time and keep your first grader from turning into a second grader, you might want to check out the next guide in this set.

Designed in partnership with Parent Cue, each guide will help you rediscover . . .

what's changing about your kid,
the 6 things your kid needs most,
and 4 conversations to have each year.

WANT TO GIFT A FRIEND WITH ALL 18 GUIDES
OR HAVE ALL THE GUIDES ON HAND FOR YOURSELF?

ORDER THE ENTIRE SERIES OF PHASE GUIDES TODAY.

ORDER NOW AT: WWW.PHASEGUIDES.COM